CONCORDANCE

Books by Susan Howe

Available from New Directions

The Birth-Mark

Debths

The Europe of Trusts

Frame Structures: Early Poems 1974–1979

The Midnight

My Emily Dickinson

The Nonconformist's Memorial

Pierce-Arrow

The Quarry

Sorting Facts; or, Nineteen Ways of Looking at Marker

Souls of the Labadie Tract

Spontaneous Particulars

That This

CONCORDANCE

Susan Howe

A New Directions Paperbook Original

PUBLISHER'S NOTE: The poem "Concordance" was originally published by the Grenfell Press in 2019, in a limited edition.

Design by Leslie Miller
Manufactured in the United States of America
New Directions Books are printed on acid-free paper.
First published as New Directions Paperbook 1480 in 2020

Library of Congress Cataloging-in-Publication Data
Names: Howe, Susan, 1937– author.
Title: Concordance / Susan Howe.
Description: First edition.
Identifiers: LCCN 2020005694 | ISBN 9780811229593 (paperback) | ISBN 9780811229593 (ebook)
Subjects: LCGFT: Poetry.
Classification: LCC PS3558.O893 C66 2020 | DDC 811/.54—dc23
LC record available at https://lccn.loc.gov/2020005694

10 9 8 7 6 5 4 3 2 1

New Directions Books are published for James Laughlin
by New Directions Publishing Corporation
80 Eighth Avenue, New York 10011

CONCORDANCE

“**SLIVER** (2)

1885 ‘An envious Sliver broke’ was a”

Concordance to the Letters of Emily Dickinson

To Abbie C. Farley early August 1885.
“‘An envious Sliver broke’ was a passage your Uncle peculiarly loved in the drowning Ophelia”

SINCE

Ghostly step pre-articulate hop

Recovering the lost is like entering enemy lines to get back one's dead for burial then to come home to Blackstone's warning of a dead hand waving *Gulliver's Travels into several remote regions of the world: in words of one syllable with fifty four illustrations*. Mortmain. Hnm is another spelling of Houyhnhnm. Whnaholm. Oliver Wendell Holmes Jr. in posthumous life is the Auto-Icon at home. A Howe is not a Holmes.

Shh, the stone hasn't been rolled from the sepulchre yet. "I have a little shadow that goes in and out with me." I learned that one by heart when my bed was a boot. 1939. Armies in the fire. Boo hoo

"See the pictures on the walls, / Heroes fights and festivals." Only friends and intimate relations call each other thou as in Keats discovering Homer. Slow time to fast time—wood to wire—what else can be expected from soaring on air pinions above others.

"Friends! I never had any friends!"

Hereinafter microscopic reduplications of desire are pieced together through grid logic. In order to facilitate phonetic interpretation I will make up my mouth as if it's a telegram.

Dark Age of Scottish Legal History 1350–1650

"Nous faisons une théorie et non un *Spicilège*." I hope you will use my house about two stories even if I'm borderline inauthentic lying. Given cross references there is no way of checking.

Puck is the only person acting Connecticut so he puts on a paper hat—Åcorn

How does a little picture look in a small frame; the side that faces the artist with its promise of happiness? Mind your own business. To back track is to retrace one's steps or to retreat. Taylor the water-poet makes use of the word rusty-fusty-dusty. 1630. Workes. Pt. ll.

Hare in oval Victorian broach don't fidget

I'm so scared of dying without answers only a phrase to use as earring or necklace—surrounded by Boston, Dublin, Killiney, Buffalo, Cambridge, Annisquam, Cotuit.

Ladder ladder fish water

Can you hold your breath under water? Call the German pediatrician. Where are we now? Why would you go away? *Nomen est omen*. Are you dead or alive? This is radio memory. I am physically weary so I will slide with the house.

Counting sheep running across meadows or driven in herds

How blind are we to futurity? All dreaming and other psychological phenomena at long distance as if to say this closet is the closest you come to Nathaniel Draper's dialogue between himself and the spirit of Benjamin Franklin as relayed through his magnetized wife

Rapping at the closet door. Wedding not a dance. Mesmerism. How did you find me middle of nowhere?

Echo echo I love you. Breathe breathe

God's prerogative. The proper time of X rev is after the end of the world for we will have finished the work of mediators.

Spirits interpenetrate—drift apart—signals and transmissions—the ins and outs, reversals, refugees, bombs, borders, children separated from parents, forced migration, mass incarceration, fracking, plastic bags, environmental destruction, possible human extinction, all the mutilations of love in time's relentless march from war to everlasting war.

"I'm dead, I'm like a ghost on the battlefield with bullets flying through me."

Holmes the Nimble

To a certain extent I'm also alive. My legal secretaries lost their way—a wrong turn of the pen—I don't know why or how. Who are you Swan Lawyer Unmarried Male Maidens begging me to stay one day longer? Now I am doomed to wander web shadow libraries. No verdict is final. Once we said genius was health now we say genius is time. I don't know any more than that. There is nothing more I can do.

Concordance can also mean a state of harmony between persons. Or a musical chord with satisfying musical effect.

High above the city on a tall column above the roar of Niagara stands the Happy Concordance with its double duplication lenses. Swallow swallow how can landscape be so flat at the border of death brother of sleep. I will stay with you always steadfast tin soldier

What is rabbit light? Is it a fusion of rabbit and light? Reversal of like and kill?

"If a man is on a plank in the deep sea which will only float one, and a stranger lays hold of it, he will thrust him off if he can. When the state finds itself in a similar position, it does the same thing."

Waves are breaking over our heads. Now come the sea liars. Betray is a single word forever revolving on its own double meaning revealing in itself a constantly shifting balance of gains and losses.

Flutter about peacock feather on wire

Skeletal affinities, compound nonsense stutters, obsolete dipthongs, joins and ellipses, homophones, antonomasia—I feel profoundly bound to you and want to wear your wigs.

In lieu of executors, please leave lexicographers

Noah Webster flaunted colloquialisms of New England as authority for correctness. *SPELL, n.* “a short time; a little time. [Not elegant.]” “WHITTLE, *v. t.* To pare or cut off the surface of a thing with a small knife. Some persons have a habit of *whittling,* and are rarely seen without a penknife in their hands for that purpose. [This is, I believe, the only use of this word in New England.]”

The speech bubble coming out of his head contains the words “I live in Divinity.”

It’s too late then to prepare for internal government in a dangerous world of false appearances while proudly falling on one knee as if begging pardon in order to signify whatever true state of the case will confirm cutting-edge happiness.

What message what sin and mistake?

"Instruct me, for Thou know'st; Thou from the first / Wast present, and with mighty wings outspread / Dovelike sat'st brooding on the vast abyss, / And mad'st it pregnant."

Brood is both noun and predicate. "Young broods are in the grass." Each in its proper place; all ready to be called to life. A spirit of inquiry has gone forth and sits here brooding.

"The Common Law is not a brooding omnipresence in the sky, but the articulate voice of some sovereign or quasi sovereign that can be identified." *Southern Pacific v. Jensen*, 244 U.S. 205 (1917)

Dissenting opinion

"Brooder, brooder, deep beneath its walls— /A small howling of the dove / Makes something of the little there, // The little and the dark, and that / In which it is and that in which / It is established." Wallace Stevens, "The Dove in Spring" *Seven Arts No. 2*, 1954

Dean Swift, Esther Johnson, Dean Delany, Mary Delany, Archdeacon Lawrence Sterne

What is belief if we betray elocution? That's why we kneel when we pray.

Who wore a garment that had no seam, John 19.

John, John, the gray goose is gone!

See how fate flies into freedom and freedom into fate. Law, Medicine, Divinity, where are we now? "Faith faith." The mistake was already made as a first vanishing act ritualized.

This far I will go and no farther into the Primal Anxiety Great Dissenter Imaginary Friend Category.

Concordances were biblical at first.

As a relic of the typewriter generation, my field is the page with its harmonics—something to do with breath and keys that puncture. I know brilliant alluring virtuosities both strange and terrible are inevitable. Faster better technologies—deep space, non-real reality—"O brave new world that has [no paper] in it."

I have to confess this anxious entry may be the only place for comprehending important concerns of so-called private life and am sending it off as an "accidental wish" in folklore.

Trusting that as a helpful reader you will respond in your rabbit self. I have composed a careful and on one level truly meant narrative and on another level the Narrative of a Scissor

Always is a reader going on with little and great hops

Sally means willow in Irish Saileach resembling Sail. "There was an old woman and she lived in the woods / weile, weile, waile / There was an old woman and she lived in the woods / Down by the river Saile" is from an old Dublin street ballad about infanticide. "She had a pen-knife / Long and sharp / weile, weile, waile / She stuck the pen-knife in the baby's heart."

Names set off phonologic sparks and echoes can be seen as rungs on a veil ladder. When the real and symbolic melt into each other is it possible for phonological spirits from another world to scatter visible shadow-mortality over the presence of the violent unknown-no-matter-what

Scissor a stricken rabbit crying out

"SCISSORS, n. *plur. siz'zors.* A cutting instrument resembling shears, but smaller, consisting of two cutting blades movable on a pin in the center, by which they are fastened. Hence we usually say, a pair of scissors."

"Life is painting a picture not doing a sum." Oliver Wendell Holmes Jr.

"Though, as we have seen, the two eyes look on two different pictures, we perceive but one picture. The two have run together and become blended into a third which we see in each." Oliver Wendell Holmes Sr. in "The Stereoscope and the Stereograph," *Atlantic Monthly*, June 1859

What if each free-moving mirror phoneme corresponds to unexpectedly unconquerable hopes descending from the symbolic relation in cipher

Mary Temple, Fanny Dixwell, Clover Hooper

I have your bags packed but might lose them. Many a young person now and then can wish to see how to go far, far off; out of reach above all all things below nacre mother of pearl where names are set down in meaning and sense of promise tangled with golden beads for stars deposited with ancestors as trespass brought home. A crescent moon is hard to see stitched apparently at random but with finest knowledge if you give to receive each transitory life and this might mean that death is not so frightening but a soaring sense of open sky a mile off distant at sea worked with every sort of thread even hair when thread is too fine for whirling snow to press down over nights with veils of iambic lines and perfect quatrains so tiny no margins calling into doubt nominal subjects less religious than decorative before professional embroiderers aggressively slashing stitches said to be not for profit dwelling in trusted digital archives only a few of us are instantly legible as with a painted sun on the wall you see the sun and stars there is a difference between. Go to a ladder that leads to free air. All things serve when the psalm sings instead of the singer.

Henry James looking both ways once.

Sometimes the short race wins. Starting now at the center singing beyond visual frames where truth as light in delight and leisure in pleasure is work never finished because art is experimental and renews. Mary (Minny) Temple as Milly Theale provides peace and pardon and will not make excuses as others do. Faith runs parallel. Innocence at abiding nothing in our world and never can be other than a ghosted self in *Wings* roaming long afternoons and open vistas among other weekend visitors at Matcham embarking with Watteau for Cythera or the campus of some great American university. Smooth ocean a bit of tossing blue water with little waves climbing for tribulation near at hand. She already turned her face to the wall so she is original always out of place in Europe despite appearance. In the close amen she has nothing. He doesn't want to put money in something so easily broken while coming back carries the burden of what mere money promises or represents only a few steps from Puritan wilderness hymns to billion dollar New York elevator glass skyscraper amplification.

Library canary hopping on twig caged peeps scratches

Here comes the scapegoat driven into the desert undo her necklace. In the Ark of the Constitution what we know and should have known

Short dream about being treated being treated badly by a professor in memory of friends and colleagues who knows why I cannot find or win. Doves as gulls carrying marriage messages breaking through initial particulars maybe this is world life saving's time from an art-historical perspective at the cusp of post-WWII and postwar Cold War Brutalism.

Clefs, chirps, upward glides, falling whistles

Covert affections persist in the soul under sleep only to meet in print where they can at least be felt by a reader. Each letter a separate presence yes but without restraining slippers.

Paul Valéry says the first line of a poem should come from the edge of things like a magic formula deep inside the chamber of a mollusc shell.

"Emily Dickinson from Judge Otis P. Lord, 1880": written on the flyleaf of her copy of *The Complete Concordance to Shakespeare: being a verbal index to all the passages in the Dramatic Works of the Poet*, edited by Mrs. Cowden Clarke, Boston: 1880.

1881. "Judge Lord— // Court House— / Boston—
"Antony's remark to a friend, 'since Cleopatra died' is said to be the saddest ever lain in Language—That engulfing '*Since*.'"

Hairline fracture above the final "Since."

14 May, 1882. "To remind you of my own rapture at your return, and of the loved steps, retraced almost from the 'Undiscovered Country,' I enclose the Note I was fast writing, when the fear your Life had ceased, came, fresh, yet dim, like the horrid Monsters fled from in a Dream. Happy with my Letter without a film of fear, Vinnie came in from a word with Austin, passing to the Train. 'Emily, did you see anything in the paper that concerned us?' 'Why no, Vinnie what'? 'Mr. Lord is very sick.' I grasped at a passing Chair. My sight slipped and I thought I was freezing. . . . Then Vinnie came out and said 'Prof. Chickering thought we would like to telegraph.' He 'would do it for us.' 'Would I write a Telegram?' I asked the Wires how you did, and attached my name."

New York Times, December 1882, "Oliver Wendell Holmes the son of Dr. Oliver Wendell Holmes was Friday appointed an associate Justice of the Supreme Court, Bench of Massachusetts in place of Justice Otis P. Lord."

Farewell Massachusetts Supreme Judicial Court. Asylum, cell, door, closet, window frame. Magical thoughts. Owl running around sheep pen

Twilight in Cotuit

Having crossed over and arrived I looked out over the oyster beds between boats and thought he will be there walking over the beach to the other summer house—but he wasn't there either. I was getting more and more anxious more and more filled with the urgency of my excuse because it was in a leather brief case. I was carrying documents as proof

Speaking of consistency, as if it could happen to your real self sitting here in your Connecticut house 2019. Whatever is needed to show who saved and who did not save.

"It is an essential part of the claim man's job to lay the foundation for the recovery of salvage, if that is at all possible." March 5, 1938, Wallace Stevens, "Surety and Fidelity Claims," *The Eastern Underwriter.*

"Old Johnny Morse years ago was asking me why my moustache was so much better than his and I replied 'It's been nourished in blood.'"

Bringing things together. Lawyers and Poets do that.

Seeking for truth In the rage darkness where the Forty-two Judges of the Dead are seated and one of the Supreme Nine weighs each heart against a feather.

Rabbit-Duck illusion

Recently I dreamed of a woman who was a dancer resembling Suzanne Farrell in an article I'd been reading about George Balanchine and his production of *Don Quixote* where he was the old man in his suit of armor though in the dream he was France. Farrell was Dulcinea but she could also be America. The dress she wore was cinched at the waist set with "white coral bells upon a slender stalk." I borrowed it and felt such happiness even if I knew I wasn't original. There I was with my scissor self so I already knew I had to give up and go on in my ordinary way roaming the ordinary streets of you guessed it, New Haven. It seemed to me then that the dress represented poetry or what you write on paper to cover yourself but you can only wear it briefly. It isn't a costume it isn't a robe. The spangled sleeves are tight at the wrists and they only outline your arms because they are transparent and your arms spread freely out like a dancer and you are young and wearing paper shoes not the red ones in the Hans Andersen story where poor Karen can't stop dancing, not Dorothy's ruby spangled ones in *The Wizard of Oz,* not the high heels Ginger Rogers wears while dancing backwards, not the toe-shoes Moira Shearer puts on in Michael Powell's film, not even the open backed slip-ons in Rembrandt's *Susanna und die beiden Alten* 1647 at the Gemäldegalerie in Berlin. That small oil on mahogany panel was owned by Sir Joshua Reynolds who altered and painted over it during the eighteenth century so Samuel Richardson may have seen it in London when he was composing and setting the type for *Clarissa*, *or, The History of a Young Lady, Comprehending the Most Important Concerns of Private Life*. I felt lucky to have made it to such a museum (even though it took until I was seventy) but at the same time sorry that Wallace Stevens never flew or sailed across the Atlantic ocean to see her here in paintflesh. Flooded in light Susanna has half taken off her rich red outer robe, and left it with the red slippers on the stone pedestal as she steps half naked into her bath that could almost be a quarry pool in the woods of the Connecticut shoreline during the early Mesozoic period, when oldest rock formations were formed. One of the peeping elders is pulling at the white cloth still loosely wrapped below her waist. He is looking at her hair and pulling the material away while the other bearded elder leaning forward on his judge's throne leers with a smile in her direction—not *quite* directly. Her startled gaze out at us her audience could simply mean "Leave me alone!" Far off, to the upper left, are the towers of what must be her husband Joakim's Babylonian palace but the swirling browns and ochres to the left almost erase the garden pool which is artificial since she is entering barefoot stepwise

Iconographia

It's even possible in the cut paper salvage clutter on my desk to call up the coffin-harpsichord-escritoire Clarissa calls her "palace" and to juxtapose them both with the red-eyed elders watching Susanna and "Peter Quince at the Clavier." "Upon the bank, she stood" "while / The red-eyed elders, watching, felt / The basses of their beings throb / In witching chords, and their thin blood / Pulse pitzzicati of Hosanna."

Susanna is Hebrew for "lily." "*My dearest Miss Howe! /* O what dreadful dreadful things I have to tell you.'" Clarissa orders the head of a lily "snapt short off and just falling from the stalk" as her coffin icon.

Robert Lovelace, Peter Quint

Down at the heel scullion of fate will never settle on something when all is passing scurry and watershine changing, nothing remains but the beauty of this sheet of paper waving like a sail scudding between phonemes and syllables as if the wind has blown a flower of the field from Pangaea in Permian time, when Earth was one continent with one Panthalassa Ocean. Google again for the source of my quotation and I'll fetch you another governess-related origin in grandmother glossolalia, kinesthetic shadowy defining other metaphoric surface-embroideries folding and fracturing retracing convoluted needlework patterns. You don't get to where you think after extensive fieldwork just for a chance to see Pangaea break apart in a process that leads to the birth of the Atlantic ocean twenty million years before the public is ready for twilight liberalism.

Temples, amphitheaters, acres of gardens. Artificial lakes and side doors. Tears of blood. Dissenters. Dinosaurs

A world without America in it rushing along the distance between now and then

Possession and dispossession

Late poems tiptoeing on a philosophical threshold of separation and mourning for an irrevocable past holding to memory, the death of memory condensed through concordance logic lit by a hidden terrain where deepest homonyms lie

Unpersuadeable

. . . things to the first institution, and observe wherein and how they have degenerated; but yet ask counsel of both times—of the ancient time, what is best; and of later time, what is fittest.

Names stand out in single isolation. Not for what they say or for what seems to remain unsaid stepping out as much as you like. Each slight verbal reference or connection gets lost though found by some inherent sense of form in every respect but touch linking the always undiscovered country to all families on earth. There is no other way Eve the unknowable author of life will live to teach others, bruising the Serpent's head from years of treading water under history. Ideas are her undercover only shells remain as placeholder keeping her spiral self safe somewhere far off she lays siege to your heart in spirit of the occult as the setting-into-the-work-as-truth made to blend others so that wrath is not the last thing, knowing birth is identical with death, and even mercy seasonable in days of affliction. This has something to do with ecology with what lies buried on the ocean floor; shields and sails and ships cast down, eons before house and home even before time as the roofed gateway in which a bier is placed before again disappearing.

You might not have an answer at the end, but you try it this way, now this way. You can't control that part of you that experiences by yourself what is familiar. The way a style begins in the name of clearness then narrows to stumbling on pavement cracks and worrying how to get up again without balance. These days I'm using Lyrica for neuropathy and Retaine for dry-eye. Across the road as butterfly weeds decline they create a swirl of twisted flower stems. I am alone in my workroom reading about *The Whole Booke of Psalmes Faithfully Translated into English Metre,* commonly known as the *Bay Psalm Book* 1640, printed by Stephen Daye, in Cambridge, Massachusetts. Apr 6. 1699.

All thy garments smell of myrrh, and aloes, and cassia. . . .whereby they have made thee glad. My beloved is unto me as a cluster of camphire.

My Antonomasia

Sea Daffodil. Six stamens and one style have been cut with such dexterity that even the anther at the end of each stamen and the stigma in the style are shown. One must cross the threshold heart of words all intricacies every particular in its minutest limit playing fast and loose encrypted for the purpose of reconciling influence the way a name spells itself and how personification leads to widow whistling at three headstones, the moths fluttering among heath and harebells. Such soothing sounds all the *h*'s and other rhythms whispering to each other on paper wondering will they ever reach seventy times seven divided into *four hundred and ninety parts* in italics.

If one could ever build a cairn to outlast the sound of cell phone ringing imagined as breath so you won't disappear poor Hareton the most wronged for doing nothing.

"Life imitates Art far more than Art imitates Life" or so says Oscar Wilde in *The Decay of Lying: An Observation*. An aphorism is a dictum perfected to the point of wit. Wit and weaving have the same beginning. "Death is the brother of Sleep, is he not?"

That's Mary Manning Howe Adams in The Cambridge Holmes for Liars. "Prepare her steeds / Paw up against the light."

Lyric, Lyrica, lyre, liar, lawyer

"Happiness not in another place, but this place. Not for another hour, but this hour." That's Walt Whitman not Wallace Stevens. Concordian serenity. Sound clusters passing through phonological nets called names but opening as if by magnet to myriad elected affinities.

"Feb. 5, Talked about Emerson again today—Holmes saying how extraordinary that 'a hen-blooded farmer-parson' could ever written such things as he did. And then he started reciting 'fired the shot heard round the world.' He described [him] as a wonderful looking sage, with his hair curling over his collar in back—'like a hawk's feathers.'"

Down at the pier waves are whipped up and breaking against No-
man's Island an offshore granite outcropping not even half an acre
wide where gunpowder used for quarrying was stored before WWI

Wren alarm calls

Wood to wire—

Intelligence

Trees listen and wait

For now, in haste

I am going to a sea strand six centuries off in search of cockle shells
for cutting ceiling silhouettes

CONCORDANCE

Saint Mary-of-the-Woods, for
proof-reading; to Professor La
est and encouragement, to Mr.
sonal interest in the printing
students who have assisted the
this work.

December 8, 1939.

A Concordances, I may remark, are
hunting down half-remembered
worthy service. They contribute n
:e history of words, and so to the
ined such assistance from them

and and and and and and and and and and and and and and and and and and and and and and and and and and

The age ha
The famous
The famous
The famous
The famous
The famous
The famous
The famous
The combat

C O N C O R D A N T

nations *concord* broke,

Among the constellation

and are ab

Thoughts

ences between word and image,
is always present, if not invited.
:xample, a dark *E* at its center wl
a tonal analogy to the darknes

Untwisted, all the finely, fibres of the
Making (Thought palpable—& Priestly

y traceable, 'tick', over the letters
dot. I thought at first that these
concluded after careful considera-
ɔre important than, so to speak,
original writer or by some other,
The Plan of the Concordance
~~dista~~darkening
: ~~western~~ skies
lies

Q M G D Z R A O U E 1
? 2 6 3 0 2 5 5 6 8 8

Omitted Words

a, am, an, and, are, at, be, been, by,
for, from, had, has, have, he, her, him,
my, no, nor, not, now, of, on, or, our,
their, them, then, there, these, they, th
we, were, what, when, where, who, wit

:an, cannot, could, did, do, does,
his, I, if, in, into, is, it, may, me,
shall, she, should, so, that, the,
is, those, thy, to, upon, us, was,
ı, would, you, your.

OMITTED ENTIRELY

(hand)

feed and shelter it; and when I
was still another behest which it
nevertheless I endured it. Why, t
which gave us our body, takes it
bear it?—I love it, says somebody
was just now saying, is it not Nat
you this very affection? But the
says, "Let it go now, and have
with it."

). The Asylum and Dormitory it see
'ere brought to the eye by a number
;epulchral Light, that held strange ne
kept its rayless Vigil." In the sixth cc
d "The fallible . . . remains fallible."
" to "At the extremity" (a change also
itence, 'Allegoric Vision feeling

ıat w. Eden or without was done
y desire of knowledge w. bounds
ıd bid the deep w. appointed
r w. them spirit lived
ɔut w. those banks where rivers
ıg ere our approaching heard w
fish w. their watery residence
pressing well the spirit w. thee
rfect w. no outward aid require
ver active w. beyond the sense
much more I feel torment w
l peace w. favour from heaven
nself the danger lies yet lies w.
e as to the power that dwelt w.
forcible w. my heart I feel the

[2] *cf.* Index, σχοῖνος (2).

microscopically the wa
again that this use of a
that it will bring in a fu
have also a meaning ir
of the word will exist i
to throw light on the
"one should continue
use a word in a new w
used previously. ¶ I

ay in which Shakespeare use
word will be perfectly proper
irther meaning not previously
ı a particular context, which w
n that place alone. I think that
extraordinary vigour of Shake
to respect the Oxford Dictiona
ay until one is fully aware of a
think that just as the ear take
word *lacuna in*
δὲ τούτοις

Full of mysterious ...

Weaving. *See* **Vision-weaving.**

al form without ... gay dreams of sunny-tin

. she *spoke*," *D.* iv. 605; "Or what was *spoke* at
spoke," *S.* v. 308; "have I *swore*," *Mi.* ix. 67;
drank your fill," *S.* vi. 323. The Participial use
's a slip. As a rule Pope avoids the use of the
rang and *sang* do not occur, and, as in Milton,
oth the Passive Participle and the Active Past

years. . . . .
Into one web of treason; all will b

Webs. The dew-drops quiver on

Further Reading

ycomore ou qu'un palmier. Si on a joué la pi
rs pouvaient être en papier ou en tissu (the soluti
ie text is a three-dimensional tree, a real tree w
asily destroy, since it has been cut down and fa
antine can be uprooted and transported more eas
lm tree. If the play was performed in January or F
have been made out of paper or fabric) (p. 147).
That's why we're here. [*Laughs*]

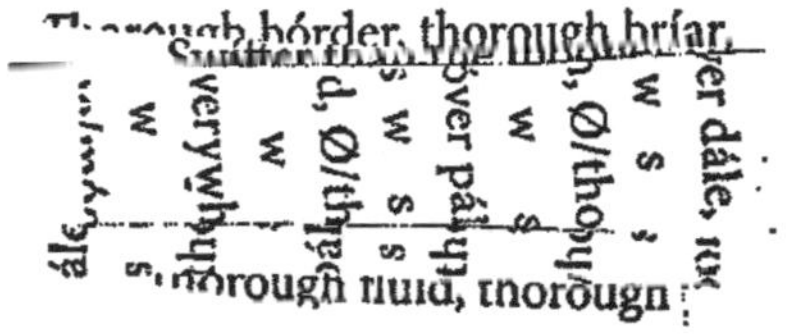
bórder, thorough bríar,
over dále,
thorough flúid, thorough
over pál
everywh

ines of the fairy's answer as a good exa

hat the moving person is the figure ar

Trajector (I, the speaker Puck [*sic*]) t

l, dale, park, pale)" (17).

discussion, this is a rath

ere are leaf-masks of va
sturbing – scattered over .
y no means unknown in the
ecorative motif in mediae
ame into their own. Some n
fe of windblown leaves; oth
vegetation springing

móonés
s
ywhere
w s w
Ø/thoro
w s
er pále
w s w
Ø/thoro
s

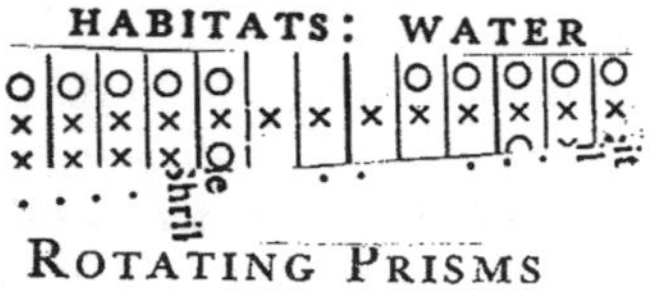
HABITATS: WATER
ROTATING PRISMS

The eternal note of sadnes
do wánder éverywhere

than the moones sphére ...
Thorough

Thetis had dark blue hair adorned
le she wore a silver shell in which two c
eils cascaded from the shell down to her
reeds. Her costume was fashioned of tl
id decorated with emblems of the sea.
veils were draped. Sh

/t/e/r/i/[illegible]
e/f/g/h/i/j/k/l/m/n/o/p/q/r/s/t/u
[illegible]

A' b A- a b A' a b A' a b A'

). Caesura may be "confirmed" by a wor

:urs in mid-word (or less critically in mid

tension, or blurring the versification nat

thorough fluid, thorough

gap of another, all empty of content as both
n described as gaps [...]". And again, "But the f
other than the absence of a feeling [...]. The r
e without a sound to clothe it [...]" (quoted by .
"struggle and, a sylla[illegible] a sim

, once subtitle
putting on, *Or the Absent-Minded:* th
ench taste, was trying, I suppose, to
singularity that Hamlet uniquely r
approaches him fades, succumbs,

Diagnostic Arrows:

ce myself out of m

ed myself to my ow

to write a poem, b

RAY-

unseen, as an author, else
es character. And he woul
r a while, make his enthusi

WORD-

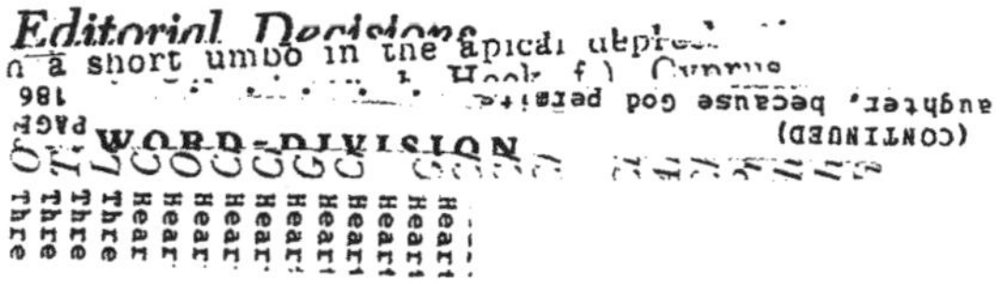
Editorial
a short umbo in the
aughter, because God
(CONTINUED)
186
PAGE
WORD-DIVISION
Thre
Hear

the sea · · · barking waves · · · the neurop

l: "and when, one day, he was found in th

ıd of a blue ribbon (because, he said, it

f the sea), the visionary had simply lost c

o Dr. Blanche's asylum." **barking wa**

· barking waves into attention", *Comus*

Γo soothe the barking waves", *Christmas*

Milton: "Like waves they me pursue", Ps

esthic winds: Apollinaire: "au vent dé

/t/e/r/i/n/m/o/d/o/i/o/n/t/r/e/e/e'

e/f/g/h/i/j/k/l/m/n/o/p/q/r/s/t/u

Lit Me Icte Les Cor Gar Bla Spc Coi Sca Bra Wh Tre Bai La Or Wr Ni Ta Sw

:e is to start a passage with a few pencill
ontinue it on the typewriter, so that I shc
pt of any poem of any length, and I nev

s/u/a/v/i
a/b/c/d/

104 *Var. Cottle, 1797,* 3
109 *Rel. Musings* 11
109] *Var. del. Rel. Mu. ings, MS. Potts,* 12
109 *Var. Rel. Musings, 1796,* 20
110 *Rel. Musings* 26
110 *Var. Rel. Musings, 1796,* 26
113 *Rel. Musings* 93
124 *Var. Rel. Musings, 1803,* 401
127 *Death of Chatt.* 5
134 *Dest. Nations* 79
142 *Var. Dest. Nations J.-A., II, 287, 4°,*

.679. death to life is c. of
9. unmindful of the c. that virtue give
978. with a c. of deathless praise

)

Λ

	— Uchrus
ὴρον τὸ)	—— sativus
ͻόφορον	—— tuberosu
ɿ.	Laurus nobil
ɼ	Lavandula sı
κιττός	Lavatera arb
ᴧόχρυσος	Lecokia creti
ɪɒ-ρόπιον	
Λ	Lemna mino
ȝορος,	Ligustrum vı
Λ ᴧο·ιέλας	Lilium candi
Λ ʻȝ ȝορίνη	
,	—— chalcedc
Λ ɥθ	
ɪο,	—— Martago
ʄəɣ κουκιόφο-	Limnanthem
) ɣ ο	phoides
(ʄəɣı	Linum usitat
Λ	Lolium temul
ιοɪɣ. ɼτρος	Lonicera etru
ρɪəɣ.	Loranthus eu
ʻȝɪɣ	Lupinus alba
ιες τὸ	Lychnis coror
ρώνειον	Lycoperdon E
ɪdə ,α ἡ θή-	—— giganteu
ɹʌəoɩ ɩ	

EDITORIAL EMENDATIONS IN THE COPY-TEXT

Plasmodiophoromycetes

And Inquisition of that scanning eye.—......

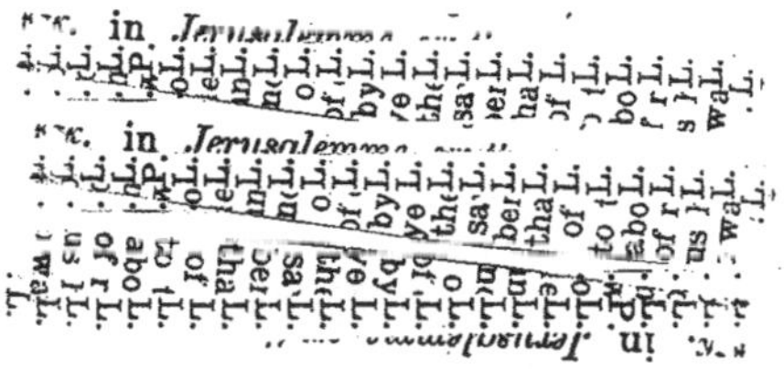

II P. 49. anc
Retirement
P. R. 4, 245.
Retires.—P. :
P.L.10,433.by
Retiring.—P
P. R. 2, 161.
P. R. 3, 164.
S. A. 16. her
Retort.—P. I
Retorted.—F
Retreat.—P.
P. L. 2, 317.
P. L. 6, 237.
P. L. 6, 799.
P. L. 10, 435.
Retreated.—
Retreating.-
Retrenched.·
Retribution.

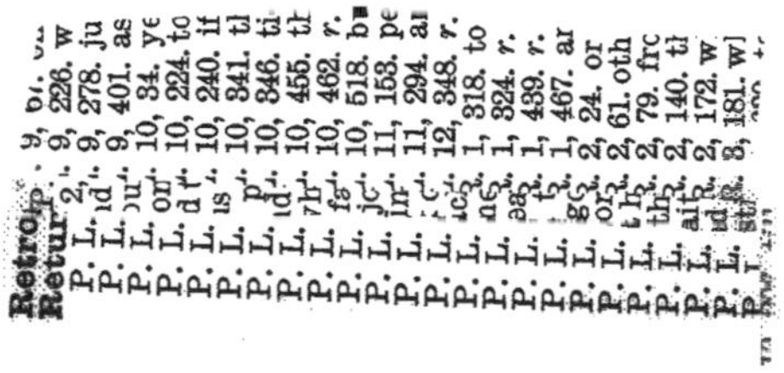
Retro
Retur
9, 226. w
9, 278. ju
9, 401. as
10, 34. ye
10, 224. to
10, 240. if
10, 341. tl
10, 346. ti
10, 455. th
10, 462. r.
10, 518. b
11, 153. pe
11, 294. ar
12, 348. r.
1, 318. to
1, 324. r.
1, 439. r.
1, 467. ar
2, 24. or
2, 61. oth
2, 79. fro
2, 140. tl
2, 172. w
3, 181. wl

. 154. prison
. 591. that these *d.* orbs no more shall
. 197. in thy *d.* lantern thus close up the stars
. 383. he that hides a *d.* soul and foul thoughts
. 500. how couldst thou find this *d.* sequestered
with curses *d.*
10. in *d.*
. 19, 2. half my days
. 123. and cast the *d.* foundations deep
. 219. in vain with timbreled anthems *d.*
7 swallowed up in *d.*
too *d.* for day to know
d. womb

What great tomb haugter has swept th(
[?No] this [?th] remains when all else
And finds there nothing to make its te

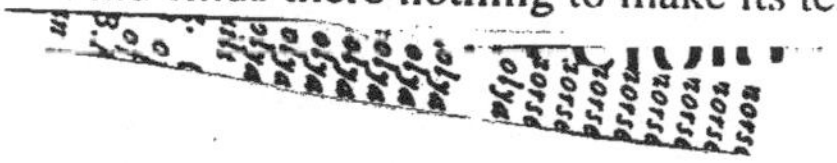

15
—, Bay-leaved
—, Bedford, 1
—, Crack, 153,
—, Creeping, 1
—, Cricket-bat
—, Dark-leave
—, Dwarf, 165
—, French, 151
—, Golden, 15
—, Lapland, 16
—, Net-leaved,
—, Sadler's, 16
—, Tea-leaved,
—, Tree, Small,
—, Weeping, 16
—, White, 156, 1
—, Whortle-leav
—, Woolly, 166
Willows, 150
Withy, 153

alphabet of stars alone does

LOST NOTEBOOK

And now the wedding day was f...

alignment, claiming to synthesize the di
uarter; or, if some façade, according to
ination, isolates, in a square, its ghost, I
what, here and there, is whispered, as a
gues of flame are turned down.

End-of-the-Line Hymenation

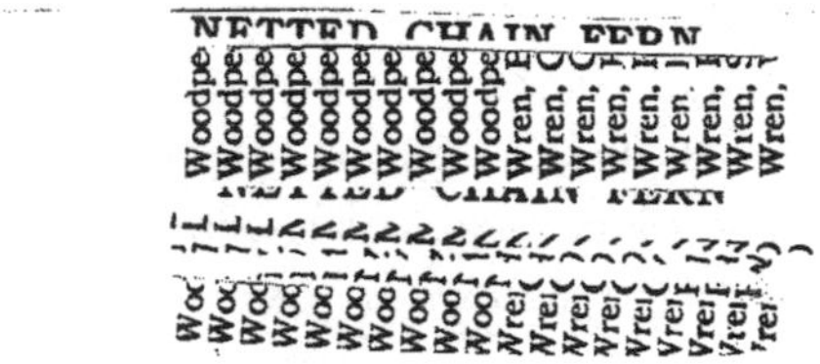
NETTED CHAIN FERN
Woodpe
Woodpe
Woodpe
Woodpe
Woodpe
Woodpe
Woodpe
Woodpe
Wren,
Wren,
Wren,
Wren,
Wren,
Wren,
Wren,
Wren,

NETTED CHAIN FERN
Woodpe Woodpe Woodpe Woodpe Woodpe Woodpe Woodpe Woodpe Woodpe Woodpe
Wren, Wren, Wren, Wren, Wren, Wren, Wren, Wren, Wren,

): THE CHARIOT OF FAMA

999] 999999999999999999999999 9999999999999999999999
999999999999999999999999 9999999999999999999999

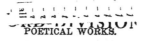

POETICAL WORKS.

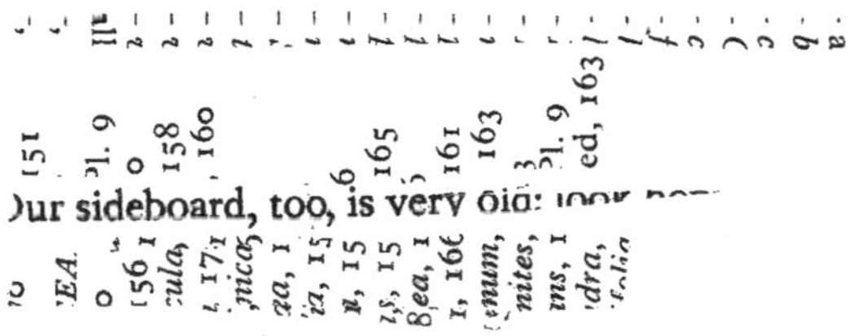
ur sideboard, too, is very

ENQUIRI

αιγιλωψ

ἀρία, ἄσπρις,
δρῦς, ἐτυμό-
δρυς, ἡμερίς,
ἴψος, πρῖνος,
σμῖλαξ (1),
φηγός, φελ-
λόδρυς, φελ-
λός
ἰξία (1)
βρόμος
part used for food
σικύα bottle gourd

Marginalia:

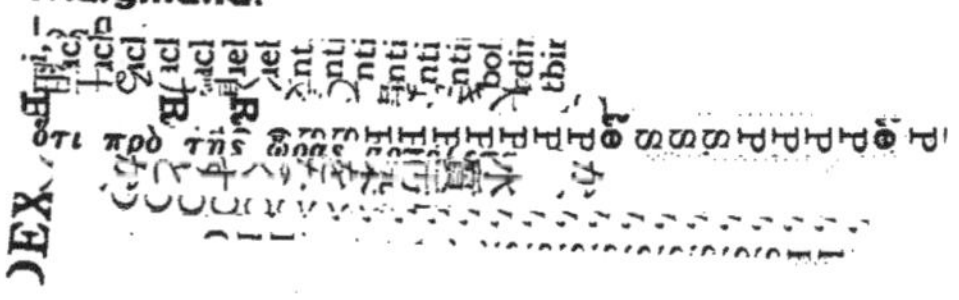

HERMIT THRUSH

Sparrow,
Sparrow,
Sparrow,
Sparrow,
Sparrow,
Sparrow,
Sparrow,
Sparrow,
Sparrow,
Sparrow,
Sparrow,
Sparrow,
Sparrow,
Sparrow,
Sparrow,
Sparrow,
Sparrow,
Sparrow,
Sparrow,
Sparrow,
Sparrow,
Sparrow,
Sparrow,
Sparrow,
Sparrow,
Sparrow,
Starling.
Swallow,
Swallow,
Swallow,

オナガ[illegible]

(ガンカモ科)

PINTAIL

L ♂75cm、♀53cm

urble urble urble urble urbler urbler urbler arbler arbler arbler arbler arbler arbler arbler arbler arbler arbler arbler, arbler, arbler, arbler, arbler, arbler, arbler, arbler, urbler, urbler, urbler, urbler,

GLAUCOUS GULL, G

-skimming Flight,

. . . I translated the Poem
ly, . . . because I wished to foi
Thought—which, when I trust
TRANSLATOR'S NOTE I wishe

) ME WAS BURD
ITE HUSH END
ITE HUSH END
IN LOVE IN TH
IN LOVE IN TI

ALL BUT THE LOUD BE
ALL THINGS BUT THE
E END: . . . .
E END: . . . .
HE END: . . . .
AND LONGS FOR THE E

tis
lla
lla
lla
lla

E.

Is dead

CORDANCE
1.3.1. (?) a typical under-shr...
2. 1. 3. propagation; 2. 4. 1.
turns into μίνθη, unless often
transplanted; 6. 1. 1. in list of
under-shrubs; 6. 6. 2. a culti-
vated under-shrub; a coronary
plant: the whole plant scented;
6. 6. 3. woody: only one form;
have no

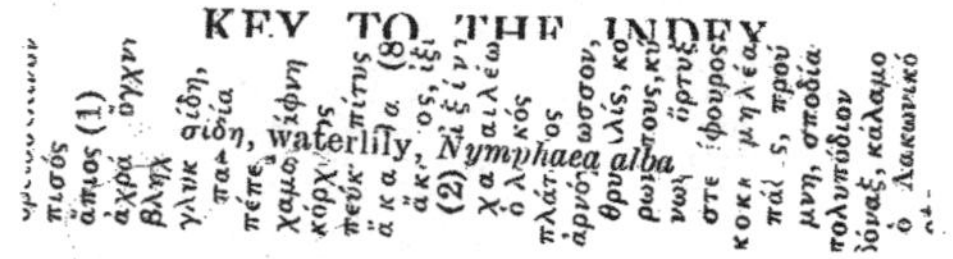
KEY TO THE INDEX
waterlily, Nymphaea alba

~~Talent~~, if ever I really possessed a
aptitude of Talent, & quickness i
enough to suffer deeply in my m
my long & exceedingly severe M
Ill-health, and partly to private aff

261 Threshold
261 Threshold
263 Threshold
263 Threshold
275 Threshold
275 Threshold
276 Threshold
276 Threshold
276 Threshold
277 Threshold
280 Threshold
280 Threshold
286 Threshold
287 Threshold
288 Threshold
288 Threshold
290 Threshold
292 Threshold
298 Threshold
301 Threshold
306 Threshold
306 Threshold
307 Threshold
309 Threshold

μενον ἀποξύ
τεῖναι. τὸ
αίοις, τούτ
ρὸς ἀλλήλ
χυτοὶ δαψι

; wings grey, under tail-covert
Some birds are more silvery-

Ralph Waldo Emerson, *Journals*, spring 1853

It is a bitter satire on our social order, just at present, the number of bad cases. Margaret Fuller having attained the highest & broadest culture that any American woman has possessed, came home with an Italian gentleman whom she had married, & their infant son, & perished by shipwreck on the rocks of Fire Island, off New York; and her friends said, "Well, on the whole, it was not so lamentable, & perhaps it was the best thing that could happen to her. For, had she lived, what could she have done? How could she have supported herself, her husband & child?" And most persons, hearing this, acquiesced in this view that, after the best education has gone far, such is the expensiveness of America, that the best use to put a fine woman to, is to drown her to save her board.

Henry James, *William Wetmore Story and His Friends*, 1903

Mrs. Story found in Rome, this and the following winter, the friend of Boston days, Margaret Fuller, whose incongruous marriage, at first, as would seem, rather awkwardly occult, had not yet offered her to the world, perhaps more awkwardly still, as Madame Ossoli; who, further, had secured and prepared apartments, and who, by this time, as a comparatively expert Roman, had, in addition to everything else, the value of a guide and introducer. At "everything else," in this lady, it would also be interesting to glance; so that, space permitting, we must not fail of the occasion.

SPACE PERMITTING

permit.

She said that mrs Hasty was 28 or 9 years old. Had her husbands likeness on her wrist & his gold watch still running when she got to the house. That mrs Hasty thought they HJh might all have been saved if they had done

Ask the painted vessel did the
Captain turn in his room what
room the storm is now raging

Preservers washed ashore ask
I can tell you nothing the vessel
went to pieces tossing planks

Now and then picking up
a hat that floated ashore
one man said the former
did not know with regard
to the sea washing their
clothes off tatters so all
at mercy of his memory
Tell me something good

Did the captain do his duty

he said he had done enough

that he was not going back

for another I don't know who

The lighthouse man said in

regard to the sea washing

her clothes off who knows—

You cannot walk on water

Saw a man with six hats on
come out and ask what now
about late parallel wars Italy
Germany the child didn't cry
to get under or over rigging
in the fitful light of common
sense drift draft experience

Tasseled dress torn by wreck—

spike lead color shut tin box

Bundle of letters and papers

a child's striped apron fringe

part calico shirt mid-print rag

and wool pocket full of sand

Thoreau's draft Hoar's copy

One man told me Bangs tore
paper part print part writing
double-eye glass thin edges

a tin box marked MF he saw
ladies' bonnets come look no
nothing trunks broken open

Orin Rose of Sayville had a

heap of rags said he would

forward a ladies shift with

the initials SMF on it rumor

Who were there first when
we got to the house to help
the latter lift up a child in
his arms but when they re-
turned for her the sea had
washed her away he saw a
silk dress lilac ground mid-

memoir extract moonstone

breast pin white nightdress

Feet on deck her chance to

force the hand of experience

Various omens looking out

Could not toss plank across

Eye glass heavy gold chain

She is not proud you cannot put
her from you because her age is
bone arid bone because of the
child in her arms its legs sticking
through to our world at least it
had just begun to walk on paper
Can you hold your breath under

She would like to live on
What has happened who
has done this I am sorry

Over here in America we
think we are free at first

I saw many leaves of a large unbound Latin book—scattered over the beach a mile from the wreck. The Universal Anatomy of Paul Mascagni Pisa 1826

Author's note:

A few notes on "Since" as well as some source texts: Robert Louis Stevenson, "My Shadow" and "Travel," *Child's Garden of Verses* (page 5); *The Common Law,* Preface, Oliver Wendell Holmes, Jr. (generally *spicilège* refers to the gleaning of a field after a harvest, but in this case it refers to the publication of historical trivia after the facts of a period have been recorded) (page 6); Oliver Wendell Holmes, Jr. to Felix Frankfurter in 1932 (page 7); regarding the "Swan Maidens"—Holmes' law clerks were called by him "Legal Secretaries" and they were required to be unmarried men (page 8); Oliver Wendell Holmes, Jr., *The Common Law* (page 9); John Milton, Book 1, *Paradise Lost*, Wallace Stevens, "Credences of Summer," *Transport to Summer,* 1947, and 244 U.S.205, 222 (1917), Oliver Wendell Holmes, Jr. dissenting (page 10); this *Concordance* was given by Judge Otis P. Lord, a Judge on the Supreme Court of Massachusetts, to Emily Dickinson: his seat, when he retired from the Bench due to illness, was filled by Oliver Wendell Holmes, Jr. (page 15); Mark deWolfe Howe, *Diary*, November 20, 1933 he was serving as Legal Secretary to Oliver Wendell Holmes, Jr.) (page 17); Oscar Wilde, "The Happy Prince," John Keats, "Sleep and Poetry," and Mark deWolfe Howe, *Diary*, February 5, 1934 (page 23).

"Space Permitting" is collaged from drafts and notes Thoreau sent to Emerson and Margaret Fuller's friends and family in Concord. They had sent him on a mission to recover her remains from the shipwreck on Fire Island. They were particularly anxious to rescue the manuscript of her recently completed *History of the Italian Revolution*. But it was lost at sea. (Read "Thoreau's Account of the Wreck of the *Elizabeth* and the Aftermath" at the online version of *The Thoreau Edition*: http://thoreau.library.ucsb.edu/resources_essays.html. Including Steve Grice, "A Leaf from Thoreau's Fire Island Manuscript," Thoreau Society Bulletin 258 (spring 2007): 1-4.)